LOVE NEVER DIES

Love Never Dies

12 Lessons I Learned About Living After Becoming a Widow

FRANKA J. BALY

Franka Baly Media, LLC.

Copyright © 2023 by Franka J. Baly

All rights reserved.

Publisher's Note: No part of this publication may be reproduced, distributed, or transmitted in any form or by any means, including photocopying, recording, or other electronic or mechanical methods, without the prior written permission of the publisher, except in the case of brief quotations embodied in critical reviews and specific other noncommercial uses permitted by copyright law. For permission requests, write to the author at franka@frankabaly.com.

Author Name
Franka J. Baly

Publisher Name
Franka Baly Media, LLC.

Contact Information
www.frankabaly.com

Cover design by Kultar Singh
Layout & Design: Franka Baly
Printed in the USA

Love Never Dies: 12 Lessons I Learned About Living After Becoming a Widow/ Franka J. Baly. – 1st ed.
ISBN 979-8-218-31344-9

Dedication

To my twin loves, Jared and Kaelen.
You've brought so much joy to my life.
I'm a better human because of you.

Contents

Letter To My Readers ix
Using This Book xi

1. Introduction: How My Grief Journey Began 1
2. Lesson 1: When you get sucker punched by life, it's okay to cry. 10
3. Lesson 2: It's okay to get mad at God—He/She can handle it. 17
4. Lesson 3: You can't run away from grieving with busyness. 25
5. Lesson 4: Prioritize your own self-care. 32
6. Lesson 5: Tell people what you need from them. 39
7. Lesson 6: Life be lifing. 46
8. Lesson 7: Invest in your own healing. 53
9. Lesson 8: Fall in love with who you are without your partner. 60
10. Lesson 9: Don't make big financial decisions when you're grieving. 67
11. Lesson 10: Love has everything to do with it. 75

12	Lesson 11: Sometimes you have to be your own cheerleader.	83
13	Lesson 12: It's important to say one final goodbye.	93
14	Final Thoughts	100

In Loving Memory	105
My Family Album	106
Citations	109
Acknowledgments	111
About the Author	113

Letter to My Readers

Dear Readers,

Fifteen years ago, at the age of 40, I became a widow. In those early days as a newly single woman and mother, navigating this seismic shift was both overwhelming and uncharted. It was made even more difficult because most women in my position were older and in different seasons of life.

As time passed, fragments of my story surfaced in my spirit, demanding revelation and acknowledgment. I began jotting down the pivotal moments as a way of preserving the raw emotions that threatened to fade with time. Moving through various seasons of life brought evolving emotions to the surface, each chapter revealing my resilience, faith, gratitude, and the enduring power of love.

Now, 15 years later, I finally feel ready to share my story. The perspective of time has given me the clarity to offer insights that may resonate with others traversing this life-altering experience.

My sincere intention in sharing this book is to extend a guiding hand to anyone who, like me, grapples with the complex array of emotions following the loss of a loved one—be it a spouse or a romantic partner (or anyone you love for that matter). Through vulnerability and shared experiences, I hope that this book becomes a companion on your grief journey.

This book is an offering, a testament to the lessons I learned during my journey with grief and loss. After each lesson, there's a place for self-reflection, gratitude, a color exercise, or for journaling your feelings and to process what arises after you finish reading. You'll be able to look back one day at what you wrote and appreciate the resilience and courage you displayed as you navigated this grief journey.

Thank you so much for choosing to embark on this process with me. May my words encourage and support you, reminding you that if I was able to emerge from the shadows of grief, you too possess the strength to navigate through them.

With heartfelt gratitude,

Franka

Franka J. Baly

Visit Frankabaly.com/loveneverdies for resources and a few other special bonuses.

Using This Book

Incorporating a daily practice that includes self-reflection, gratitude, art, and journaling greatly facilitated my healing when I was on my grief journey. My hope is that it will do the same for you. Use this book as a companion to navigate the waves of grief as they ebb and flow into your life.

To get the most out of this process I recommend that you set aside 10 - 15 minutes of quiet time to sit and reflect after reading each lesson. This will ensure you have ample time to complete the four strategies presented at the end of each chapter.

1. Self-reflection: Refers to sitting with yourself, taking an honest moment to think about what transpired, what worked, what didn't, what can be done, and what can't. Requires quiet time.
2. Gratitude: For you to indicate ONE thing you are grateful for that day.
3. Coloring Exercise: Selected images designed to help you focus your energy in a calming and creative way.
4. Journaling: The process of writing down your feelings is healing.

Each of these strategies has been proven to be effective in helping individuals to lead more fulfilled and joyful lives. I know if you commit to utilizing the strategies in this book it will help you process the avalanche of emotions you may be feeling. Each of these strategies allows for honest introspection and healing on your journey.

Recommendation: For the coloring exercise at the end of each chapter I recommend the use of colored pencils instead of markers. This will ensure that they don't damage the pages of your journal.

I love Amazon Basics Premium Colored Pencils, Soft Core, 24, 48, or 72 Count, Pack of 1, which starts at $8.35. The more colors you buy, the more you can infuse life into the images at the end of each chapter.

I'm excited to see what you will create. If you use social media I would love to see your designs. Please tag me with the hashtag #loveneverdies so I can see where your creativity took you. I know you will create something beautiful, unique, and special.

All coloring images in this book have been AI-generated using Midjourney.

Chapter 1

Introduction: How My Grief Journey Began

7:00 a.m. I woke up to the ringing of the cell phone. Sleep still in my eyes, I felt around on the nightstand for the phone and put it to my ear.

"Hello."

It was a call from my friend and pastor, Herb, but everyone called him Rev.

"Hey, Rev. What's up?"

"What are you doing today after you drop the boys off at daycare?"

"Just working on some projects."

"Can Dee come and spend the day with you?"

"Of course, I would love that. I'll call you when I'm on my way back from dropping the boys."

"Okay, see you later."

I found his request odd, but I loved spending time with Dee, so I didn't think about it too long. It was one of the perks of owning my own business; I could arrange my day however I wanted.

The clock now said 7:15, so I quickly jumped out of bed, realizing I was late getting the boys ready for preschool. I had to get them there before 8:00 a.m. Just then, one of my twins ran into the room.

"Morning Mommy!"

My Jared was always my early morning alarm. "Hi, Sweetie. Where's your dad? Is he still upstairs asleep?"

"No, Mommy, he's not home; he left already."

"Oh, okay, let's get dressed and get you to school."

The previous evening, Raphie had told me he was going in to work late that morning, so I expected him to still be home to help me with the boys. He had retired to the media room to watch ESPN when I went to bed, and I distinctly remembered him saying that he had switched his schedule with another coworker and was going in later, so I was a little irritated that he wasn't home. We had stayed up late entertaining friends for the Memorial Day holiday, and I was very tired when I went to bed. I was disappointed as I realized I didn't get to say goodbye to him before he left for work that day.

At 7:35 a.m., I got the boys situated in the car, and we headed off to their preschool. It was a beautiful and clear day. On the road, I passed a bunch of mail flying all over the street—not too much, but enough that it caught my eye and prompted me to wonder how that happened. Just as we turned onto the side street leading up to my boys' preschool, out of the blue, my son Jared asked,

"Mommy, did Daddy's brother die?"

Taken aback, I paused and then said, "No, sweetie, Daddy's brother is fine. He lives in California.

Casually, he then asked, "Mommy, did my Daddy die?"

His question floored me. Why was he asking such things? My other son, Kaelen, got upset and said, "No, Jared. Daddy didn't die. Why are you asking that?"

Calmly, I said, "No honey, your Daddy is fine. He just went in to work early. I will call him on the way home and check on him, and we'll call him when I pick you up this afternoon so you can talk to him."

"Okay, Mommy."

There was something about the way Jared asked me about the death of his father that made me very uneasy. As if he was privy to something I was not. But he was four, and four-year-olds ask questions about unusual things all the time. This time was no different, I hoped.

I pulled into the daycare and got my two guys off to their classes. I hugged and kissed them both and told them I would see them later. They happily went off to school.

I couldn't wait to get back in the car so I could call Raphie to see why he left so early that day instead of what he told me.

I called the post office station where he worked as a supervisor. His coworker answered the phone.

"May I please speak to Baly?"

"Mrs. Baly?"

"Yes."

"Has anyone spoken to you today?"

"No"

"Hold on a minute, please."

The next words uttered sent chills down my back. "Mrs. Baly, this is Mrs . . . there's been an accident . . ."

I started shaking so hard that I don't know how I drove home, and I don't remember anything else that was said to me. I have tried to recall the conversation many times, but nothing comes to mind. Somehow, I managed to call my best friend Yolanda and my brother George. I told them something bad had happened to Raphie, and I needed help.

Cars must have a memory because somehow mine found its way home. When I pulled into my driveway, my friend Rev and his wife Dee were already parked in front of our home waiting for me. As I pulled into the driveway, my immediate thought was to find out what had happened to Raphie and how bad his injuries were from the accident.

When Rev saw me pull into my driveway, he and Dee got out and walked toward me.

I walked over to them, and the words tumbled out of me one after the other without taking a breath.

"Rev, was Raphie in an accident? Did something happen to him? Is he okay? Why did they call you instead of me?"

He looked at me, and before he even uttered a word, I knew it was bad.

He looked directly at me, his voice cracking a little, *"I am so sorry, sweetie, but he's gone."*

All the air went out of my lungs, and I gasped for air. It felt like someone suddenly punched me in the stomach. I crumbled to the pavement, unable to hold up the weight of my body, and I let out a piercing wail in the middle of the driveway.

"Noooooooooooo no, no, no," I cried.

Several of my neighbors came out of their homes, curious about the commotion. I don't remember who said what. There was murmuring and lots of nodding. Everything else was a blur. Exactly like the sound the adults make in an episode of Charlie Brown. *"Wah-Wah-Wah."*

Right at that moment, the world started spinning. All I wanted to do was lie down. I wanted the spinning to stop, and it felt like I was floating in a dream sequence.

I thought, *"This is not happening. This is not really happening. Is this really happening? Could this be happening?"*

My friends must have noticed that I looked confused because they helped me inside so I could sit down on the sofa. I sat dazed and in shock as the tears continued to fall.

It was then that Yolanda arrived. Then, minutes later, my brother arrived. I relayed the awful news as tears streamed from my eyes. They were both visibly shaken.

A short while later, friends and family started arriving at our home. I didn't know how they all knew what had happened so fast. It was overwhelming how many people were now crowded into our little home. Everywhere I looked, there were people. On top of that, the doorbell kept ringing. People kept asking if I needed anything.

I didn't know what I needed. I didn't want to need anything. I wanted to turn back time.

It was then that I remembered Jared's questions from the morning on the way to school.

The memory of it still gives me chills. Had he sensed that his father had passed? Even stranger was that Raphie died close to where Jared had asked his questions, on a road we traveled every morning on the way to their preschool. The remnants of mail I had passed in the road marked where the accident had taken place earlier that morning. Just minutes from our home.

Then, all I wanted was to get to my boys. To tell them what happened to their dad and how wrong I was this morning when I told them everything was fine. I didn't know I was giving them wrong information and how sorry I was that they no longer had their Daddy. I needed to hug them, but I didn't trust myself to drive.

Yolanda offered to go get them.

I thanked her.

I sat back down.

My brain registered what Rev had told me about Raphie being gone, but a part of me didn't believe him. I fully expected Raphie to walk through the door and say that it was all a terrible joke.

He would utter that memorable boisterous laugh of his and exclaim, "Ha, haaaa!"

But it wasn't April, and there were no fools around.

I watched the door expectantly, knowing that the one person I wanted to walk through it wouldn't be. I longingly wished he would. He would never leave his family. He loved us. He was crazy about his boys. But this had to be a terrible mistake. This was NOT happening to us.

But it was. It truly was.

My mind went to Raphie's mother. I couldn't imagine how I would tell her that Raphie, her only biological child, the person I knew she had given her all to, was no longer here. I couldn't bear to call her. To break her heart like that. I couldn't bring myself to tell her such terrible news. So, I did the only thing I could: I asked my friend Rev to relay the terrible news. As a Pastor, I felt he could tell her what I could barely dare to speak. What I couldn't yet grasp.

"Please, Rev, will you call Raphie's mother for me?"

"Yes, of course."

"Thank you."

He went into another room to make the call, but when he returned, I knew it was bad.

He told me what I already knew. That she took it hard. That it broke her heart. That she would never be the same. It was all wrong. All out of order. We don't bury our children. Our children bury us.

I was still crying. Not uncontrollably, but a steady stream of tears fell from my eyes. Enough that my brother, who was also in shock, told me to stop crying. I tried to comply. I blew my nose and silently prayed, *"God, please help me to be strong. Help me to endure what I'm about to go through."*

Losing both my parents before my 26th birthday meant that I was no stranger to loss. I worked at a cancer hospital where I lost patients all the time. Somehow, this was different.

Sudden. Jolting. This was the man I had chosen to spend my life with. The man who was to be by my side to raise our beautiful boys. He was only 41. Young and healthy. Our boys were only four. We waited 11 years to become parents. Eleven years! Now this.

My mind searched for answers to make sense of it. Why did this happen? How could I be both mother and father to my two beautiful little boys? Boys need their fathers.

I had lots of questions and no answers. The answers would come, but it would take time. Not that day. Nothing that day but questions.

This is how I became a widow at 40.

Chapter 2

Lesson 1: When you get sucker punched by life, it's okay to cry.

"Grief is a curious thing when it happens unexpectedly. It is a band-aid being ripped away, taking the top layer off a family. And the underbelly of a household is never pretty, ours no exception."

-Jodi Picoult

If you've ever participated in a funeral in America, then you know it's a process that is, for lack of a better analogy, like buckling into the Texas Cyclone rollercoaster at Six Flags for several continuous days.

Being the last of nine, I was fortunate that all of my siblings were able to travel for the funeral. They flew in from New York, Boston, Philadelphia, and St. Croix. Everyone was present to stand with the boys and me during that difficult time. My sisters, who I consider a force of nature, could singlehandedly organize anything with panache and class. I knew they would ensure that anything I needed would get done the right way, and they did.

I don't remember spending as much time as I would have liked with each of them as I was preoccupied and busy planning the details of Raphie's homegoing.

There was so much to be done, and I was consistently crossing off tasks one by one:

- Meet with the funeral home.
- Locate Raphie's DD214 (his military paperwork).
- Get funds from the bank to pay the funeral home.
- Find pictures for the program.
- Design the funeral program.
- Make a funeral playlist.
- Go to the printer to pick up the poster for the wake.
- Organize the wake.
- Get outfits for the boys.
- Find something to wear.
- Pick out clothes for Raphie to wear.

These were decisions I didn't think I would have to make for at least another four decades, yet here I was, making them.

I believe there was a little bit of madness in me in those seven days as we planned Raphie's funeral, mostly due to a lack of sleep. No matter how much I tried, any form of quality sleep eluded me.

When the day of the funeral finally arrived, my stomach was in knots—a mixture of dread and relief. Add to that my exhaustion from not sleeping and being overwhelmed by my thoughts, and I felt like I was on the verge of a nervous breakdown.

As we headed out for the funeral, I was keenly aware that from that day forward, my life would never be the same, and the lives of my children would never be the same.

As the video montage of Raphie's life flashed on the screen to the song "Don't Cry for Me" by CeCe Winans, her stirring words had a gut-wrenching effect on everyone in attendance. As I looked around the room, everyone was quietly crying or appeared to be visibly moved. You could hear a pin drop. It was the effect I wanted as we honored a life cut short.

By the time we got to the burial site, I was having problems steadying my nerves. I felt feeble and a bit shaky. I thought, *"Just a bit longer, Franka. Hang in there."*

As the rifles fired the gun salute, my heart began to pound so loudly that I thought everyone could hear it. By the time they handed me the American flag and thanked me for Raphie's service, I knew I was nearing the worst part of the day, the lowering of his casket into the ground.

It was at that precise moment that a sense of panic rose up in me. In a scene reminiscent of *The Best Man Holiday*, when Lance says goodbye to Mia, I rushed to Raphie's casket. Secretly urging him not to go and to be like Lazarus and to rise and walk.

He did not.

At that moment, as the tears overwhelmed me, my brother Erwin stepped in and gently guided me away. I wept for the finality of it all as I glanced at his final resting place one last time.

> When you lose a partner or someone you love or have loved deeply, it's *absolutely* okay to cry. In fact, it's cathartic and healing. Don't hold in the tears. Let them flow freely.
>
> You've just been sucker punched, and there's nothing to prepare you for what you're feeling. Allow yourself the space to cry until you can't cry anymore. To release the flood of emotions that have been bottled up inside.

I cried until my head ached, and finally, on that seventh day, I was finally able to rest my mind and body.

Crying is cathartic. It's healing.

Grief has its own timeline; give yourself the grace to navigate it. And yes, keep the Tylenol handy—it's sure to be a bumpy ride.

Lesson 1 Reflection

Date:_____

Today I Feel (Circle Your Choice):

1 - Joyful	2 - Happy	3 - Okay	4 - Sad	5 - Angry
😃	☺	😐	☹	😠

Today I'm grateful for:

_____

_____

_____

_____

Coloring Exercise "Memories In Bloom": This image represents the beauty that exists in the memory of your beloved. The memories you created will always remain in your heart and no time or space can diminish this fact.

Fig. 1. An AI-generated image of an open book with flowers.

Prompts: *Did you have a hard time crying after your loss? If you did, give yourself time and space to sit with your grief. How do you feel in this moment? What comes up for you as you think about your beloved?*

Chapter 3

Lesson 2: It's okay to get mad at God—He/She can handle it.

The American ritual of three days of mourning (in my case, it was six) demanded that we all return to our routines. So, as routine required, everyone retreated back into their regular lives after the funeral.

This ritual pays no attention to the fact that planning the funeral doesn't allow ample time for grieving. That comes later. So, after the rollercoaster we'd been on for six days, we were confronted with our new reality. That of a family of three.

Since Raphie had been a true workaholic, often absent due to his priorities and demanding commitments, I had grown accustomed to managing things on my own. Similar to the 10 years Michelle Obama referenced where she couldn't stand Barack, we were in that same rough early child-rearing years when most of the responsibilities fell on me and I didn't much like it nor did I like Raphie much. I side-eyed him often. This imbalance of responsibilities meant that my days were consumed with caring for our boys, running the household, and managing the finances. The saving grace for me was that I was more prepared than many when Raphie died, and this brought me some semblance of relief.

Yet, what caught me off guard were the surges of anger that welled up within me directed at God. Praying became impossible; every attempt led to silence. I consider myself a woman of faith, raised to find solace in prayer, yet I could not. Whenever I closed my eyes, there was only emptiness. I felt like I was floating in a void of nothingness.

I didn't want to be angry with God, but anger was a constant friend.

I'd read about the six stages of grief—denial, anger, bargaining, depression, acceptance, and meaning—and knew this was a normal part of the process. Yet, I despised my predictability.

Eventually, I came to realize that the best course of action was to embrace the anger, to let it be. I allowed myself to bask in self-pity. Telling God precisely why I was angry and how deeply betrayed I felt. I laid it all bare, railing against God for months on end.

I had questions that needed answers.

- Why didn't you save Raphie? Why did you let him die?
- Why condemn my boys to grow up without their father?
- Why was I chosen for the role of a widowed mother?
- What had I done to deserve this new reality?
- We had waited eleven long years to become parents. Why now?
- Could I ever guide my boys into men as both mother and father?
- Would I ever feel complete again?
- Would I ever find love again?

When the answers didn't come as quickly as I wanted, I went on a journey to find them for myself. I devoured books on loss and stories about people who claimed to have experienced heaven. I wanted to know that all my loved ones were in a beautiful place, free from any pain or sorrow. In those days, there weren't many books on becoming a widow, so it was hard to find resources that spoke to my journey. Which made it even more difficult to navigate.

In hindsight, I think my anger at God was a deflection of how angry I also was at Raphie. Yes, I said it. I was angry at Raphie. How dare he leave me! Leave us!! I had so many things I wanted to yell at him about. Like...

Why wasn't he wearing his seatbelt when he died?

Why was he driving tired when he knew he had sleep apnea and was prone to falling asleep at the wheel?

Why didn't he come to bed instead of going up to watch ESPN the night before so I could see him before he left for work that day?

Why did he give so much of his time to his job -- giving us, his family the short end of the stick?

Why did you leave us to pick up the pieces of our lives without you?

But he wasn't here anymore and I couldn't confront him with my feelings, unreasonable as they were. Truth was, I felt cheated as I sat with the jolting reality of it all. I wanted to yell at him for leaving me to navigate this journey of life alone when we signed up to do it together. I didn't know our time would be so short. We took it for granted that we would have more time. It hurt.

As I tried unsuccessfully to push away the feelings of anger that threatened to consume me, it was then that **I discovered the power of gratitude**. It began quite accidentally. I think it was because I grew wary of feeling emotionally depleted each day. So it became a part of my routine. I arose each day, grabbed my journal, and wrote down what I was grateful for in my life. That simple practice of starting my day by saying thank you for the little things shifted things for me, and something amazing started to happen. I began to feel comforted. It felt like an invisible hug and being enveloped in loving arms. Slowly, and gradually, my anger began to leave my body.

I think that's what this scripture means, "Blessed are those who mourn, for they shall be comforted" (Matthew 5:4).

> So, you see, despite my anger, God could bear it. More than that, it helped me process my anger in a healthy way. I realized that it was okay, even normal, to feel angry towards my beloved. Being authentic with my feelings allowed me to not only navigate my anger but to ultimately get to a place of genuine honesty as I grieved. Not only could God bear it, but God was prepared to stay with me through the process so I could find my way, in my own time, back to a place of joy and peace.

God knew it would be a process. One that required time and patience, and frankly, God has that in spades.

Lesson 2 Reflections

Date:_____

Today I Feel (Circle Your Choice):

1 - Joyful	2 - Happy	3 - Okay	4 - Sad	5 - Angry
😄	🙂	😐	🙁	😠

Today I'm grateful for:

_____

_____

_____

_____

Coloring Exercise "A Beacon of Light": Lighthouses symbolize strength, safety, and resilience. Qualities that enable human beings to overcome life's most formidable challenges and obstacles. Let this hopeful image encourage you.

Fig. 2. An AI-generated image of a lighthouse on a hill by the ocean.

Prompts: *Have you given yourself permission to embrace and express anger in the wake of losing your beloved? Take a moment to explore the depths of your emotions, allowing yourself the freedom to feel and process any frustration or resentment you're feeling right now, whether toward God or anyone else.*

_____

_____

_____

_____

_____

_____

_____

_____

_____

_____

_____

_____

_____

Chapter 4

Lesson 3: You can't run away from grieving with busyness.

One thing Black women know how to do—is get things done. The strong Black woman trope is simply a part of who we are. We are *magic* after all, *aren't we*?

Up until recently, I didn't realize how detrimental or toxic it could be to our mental health to embrace the notion that we could go without stopping. Without rest. I don't think I have ever given myself permission to sit with any form of trauma or pain.

I now know this is a learned behavior.

I don't think I have ever seen any woman in my life openly process pain. I have only seen *strong*. Even when they were suffering, it was done in silence.

So, after the death of my husband, I jumped into caretaking and being "head of household." I didn't take much time to stop and process anything, let alone the fact that I was hurting. What is grieving supposed to look like? Who has time to stop and be sad when you have two little ones to provide for?

So, I busied myself with a multitude of projects. One after the other.

I was handling things. Like a boss!

Or was I?

A year to the date, on the anniversary of Raphie's passing, the weight of it all nearly brought me to my knees. Silently, I teetered on the edge of a breakdown, only confiding in my dear friend Yolanda. Yolanda, in her grace, stepped in to care for the boys as I woke up that day sobbing uncontrollably. My tears flowed, not only for the loss of my husband but for the life I had envisioned and the loneliness of navigating motherhood without a partner to share the load of raising two innocent souls into adulthood.

Grief, my dear, has its own peculiar way of surfacing, whether immediately or years after the loss. Back then, I denied myself permission to grieve openly, fearing it would be seen as a sign of weakness, a crack in the façade of the strong Black woman I believed I needed to be.

I'm already a sensitive person, and I didn't see the benefit of spending time speaking to a counselor or processing my grief. I thought I had it handled. Until it handled me.

For me, grief manifested in numerous ways. From trouble sleeping to bouts of depression, I navigated all of the various ways it showed up in my life.

Here are some other ways it may manifest:

- Socially withdrawing
- Trouble thinking or concentrating.
- Becoming restless and anxious at times
- Loss of appetite
- Looking sad
- Feeling depressed
- Dreaming of the deceased (or even having hallucinations or "visions" in which you briefly hear or see your beloved)
- Losing weight
- Having trouble sleeping
- Feeling tired or weak
- Becoming preoccupied with death or events surrounding death
- Searching for reasons for the loss (sometimes with results that make no sense to others)
- Dwelling on mistakes, real or imagined, that you made with your beloved
- Feeling guilty for the loss

- Feeling alone and distant from others
- Expressing anger or envy at seeing others with their loved ones

So you see, true strength, my dear, emerges from the depths of healing. As you navigate your way through this sea of grief, you will not only be all that you can be for yourself but also for those who need you the most.

> Here's what I now know. You must honor and process your pain. Whether through the guidance of a therapist, the solace of a grief group, the support of a community, or the sacred act of journaling. It's important to let your emotions flow until a new path forward reveals itself. There's no time limit on this sacred journey; take all the time you need. Be patient, releasing any expectations of what healing should look like. This is your journey, no one else's.

Lesson 3 Reflections

Date:_____

Today I Feel (Circle Your Choice):

1 - Joyful	2 - Happy	3 - Okay	4 - Sad	5 - Angry
😄	🙂	😐	🙁	😠

Today I'm grateful for:

_____

_____

_____

_____

Coloring Exercise "Releasing Stress": The image of these balloons being released should encourage you to do the same to anything that is causing you undue stress. Give yourself grace for whatever you're going through right now.

Fig. 3. An AI-generated image of releasing a bunch of balloons.

Prompts: *Take a moment to ponder if you harbor preconceived notions about what grieving needs to look like. Have you allowed yourself to process the impact of your loss? Be honest with yourself about whether you've granted yourself the space to feel the pain, for it is in that space that healing begins.*

Chapter 5

Lesson 4: Prioritize your own self-care.

The year after Raphie's death, I failed a stress test.

I was 40 at the time.

I ended up having to schedule an angiogram so they could examine what was going on with my heart.

I remember feeling so scared, not for myself, but for my boys, who had lost their dad the previous year.

I thought to myself, "God, what's going on? Are you now going to take away their mom?"

Unexpected as it was, all I wanted was to get it over with. Coincidentally, the test was scheduled on my 41st birthday. I remember that as I got messages from family and friends with happy birthday wishes, it was mixed with an overwhelming sense of trepidation and fear that I could have complications and die on the surgical table.

Luckily, my friend Rev wouldn't allow me to entertain such negative thoughts. He assured me that it was a very common procedure and complications were rare, especially for someone my age. After he and Dee calmed me down, they sat and prayed with me to steady my nerves. As we waited quietly in pre-op until it was my turn, a sense of peace descended upon me, and I knew everything was going to be alright.

When I woke up in recovery, I silently thanked God for taking care of me. The doctor said that everything went well and there was no evidence of heart disease; my heart was healthy. There was no explanation for what was going on with my heart or why my vitals had been so erratic.

For me, there was only one conclusion: I was so anxious and sad that it was affecting my heart. The physical manifestation of a broken heart and from not taking care of myself since Raphie's death. It was likely that I had developed Takotsubo cardiomyopathy or "Broken Heart Syndrome", a condition when the heart muscle becomes suddenly stunned or weakened. It mostly occurs following severe emotional or physical stress. It's usually temporary and most people recover within a few months. I was fortunate to be one of those people. The message, "Franka, take better care of yourself; you're all your boys have now."

Message received.

Physical manifestations of grief result from the intricate connection between our emotional and physical well-being. Until this wake-up call, self-care was a distant notion. It was all I could do to drag myself out of bed each day. A radical act of self-love during the mourning period is to continue caring for yourself.

Not necessarily in this order, but it's important to . . .

- Get quality sleep.
- Move your body.
- Relax your mind.
- Rejuvenate your spirit.

Your goal is to resist the urge to succumb to grief by remaining stagnant—which may look like lying in bed all day watching Netflix, because, trust me, the temptation is real.

When Raphie left this world, the responsibility of caring for my boys became my anchor. Caring for them meant that I couldn't stay in bed all day. I needed to create a sense of normalcy for them, a routine. I forced myself to get up every day to make breakfast, take them to school, help them with homework, play with them, shuttle them to play dates, make dinner, and oversee bath time and bedtime rituals. Taking care of my boys became my saving grace.

So, I beg you—move, even if it's for just a few minutes, each day. This could be as simple as stretching in your room as you take some deep breaths or going for a walk in the fresh air.

It's what moved me closer to reclaiming my sense of well-being after my loss. I settled into the rhythm of my routine. Not just for the boys, but for my own sanity. In this routine, I summoned the courage to rediscover who I was while reclaiming my health.

When I couldn't fathom or fully process the pain of our loss, my routine became my lifeline, an intrinsic part of my daily existence.

> And so, I encourage you to embrace the beauty of routine with a special focus on your self-care. It may just be the lifeline you need, gently guiding you through the waves of grief toward rediscovering who you are.

Lesson 4 Reflections

Date:_____

Today I Feel (Circle Your Choice):

1 - Joyful	2 - Happy	3 - Okay	4 - Sad	5 - Angry
😁	☺	😐	☹	😠

Today I'm grateful for:

_____

_____

_____

_____

Coloring Exercise "Selfcare Sanctuary": As you color this photo, I want think about the importance of prioritizing self-care and how it can heal your heart as you blossom into the new you without your beloved.

Fig. 4. An AI-generated image of a comfy chair surrounded by books.

Prompts: *Are you experiencing any symptoms that are unusual for you and feel like they could be physical manifestations of your grief? How are you prioritizing self-care as you navigate through your grief journey?*

_____

_____

_____

_____

_____

_____

_____

_____

_____

_____

_____

_____

_____

_____

_____

Chapter 6

Lesson 5: Tell people what you need from them.

A part of the **strong Black woman trope** is not asking for what you need. I didn't realize how badly it was ingrained in me until I lost my husband.

This strong Black woman trope teaches us that we are:

- Natural nurturers, channeling our strength into helping others, sometimes even to the point that we disregard our own needs.
- That adversity is a source of inner power.
- Selfless strength personified, the human embodiment of the maxim that what doesn't kill you makes you stronger.

I was raised to be one of these **strong Black women**. I was taught to take care of myself. To be *"magic."* But the truth is, it was an exhausting load to carry as I navigated my grief journey.

When people reached out, I was polite but didn't know how to ask for the support I truly needed. I literally couldn't form my lips to ask for anything—sometimes because I didn't know what I needed and other times because my needs were so great that I feared it would overwhelm the person offering to help. Plus, my good manners and self-reliance wouldn't allow me to ask people to show up for me and my boys if I felt it was inconvenient for them in any way. I looked at everyone's life and made decisions for them without ever having an authentic conversation.

My immediate thoughts were . . .

- *They don't have time to help me—they're busy.*
- *They live far away.*
- *I don't want to be an imposition.*
- *This is my responsibility; I must figure it out myself.*

I did figure it out eventually, but for years, it was hard. There were no alternating weekends for me, like my divorced friends. I was with my boys all the time, 24/7—trying my best to help them navigate the challenges they faced as they grew into young adults, replete with all the demands of guiding boys who needed their dad.

A mother will do her best, but she's not a father. We're equipped very differently. Many times, I missed the bass in

Raphie's voice and the ease with which he could get the boys to comply with his wishes when it took me multiple tries to get the same result.

If I could have a redo, I would make sure that I was persistent in finding my boys positive male role models that would be in their lives as they grew into young adulthood. Someone who could be a consistent and positive influence in their lives. Whether that meant staying on the waiting list of Big Brothers Big Sisters, being persistent in seeking out mentors at my church or connecting with non-profit organizations, like 100 Black Men, who provide mentorship and support.

Although both my boys played sports, Kaelen more competitively than Jared, there were no men who took an interest in being a part of their lives on a deeper level. That person that my boys could jump on the phone with and call because they knew he would give them sage advice. Fostering that type of relationship requires consistency and time, and there was no men that played that role in their lives when they were younger. Even when people know you're a widow, they try not to assume what your needs are. It falls on your shoulders to recognize and identify your needs and then take steps to get support, whether for your children or yourself.

> To take this a step further, tell people what you need as soon as you identify those needs. Stop trying to be so strong, and don't hide your authentic struggles from the people who most need to see them. If I could share one regret, that would be it.

The blessing in this lesson, hard as it was for me to learn, is that as my children grew, they started to ask for what they needed. They either sought it out themselves, or they were exposed to men who stepped up for them through their friendships and close relationships. Jared asked for therapy when he was struggling with anxiety and depression after the pandemic. Kaelen started attending a church where he found community, love, and several men who became invested in his success. For his senior prom, I didn't have to spend a penny because his mentor took him shopping for his entire outfit. This is what happens when you vulnerably share your struggles with people who care. But even if you don't, God has a way of showing up for you and giving you exactly what you need when you least expect it. I call it a God-wink.

So, I want to encourage you to tell people what you need from them. Don't be too proud to ask for help. Most importantly, don't try to manage anyone's responses. **Just ask**. The worst they can say is "*no,*" and trust me, that's NOT the worst thing you'll ever hear on this journey.

Lesson 5 Reflections

Date:_____

Today I Feel (Circle Your Choice):

1 - Joyful	2 - Happy	3 - Okay	4 - Sad	5 - Angry
😄	🙂	😐	🙁	😠

Today I'm grateful for:

_____

_____

_____

_____

Coloring Exercise "The Bees": As you color this photo, think about the interconnectedness of all life. Without bees, we wouldn't have much of our food. Seeing ourselves as interconnected is both humbling and empowering: There is strength in learning to lean on others.

Fig. 5. An AI-generated image of bees pollinating flowers.

Prompts: *What are some areas in your life you need support for? This is your time to get real. Is there anyone you can ask to support you in fulfilling those needs? Make a list of your needs and the best person to help you in meeting those needs.*

Chapter 7

Lesson 6: Life be lifing.

Leading up to and after the funeral, a lot of people will tell you that they'll be there for you. I've learned it's the polite thing to say. They do it out of habit, pity, sorrow, their own grief—a multitude of reasons cause people to offer unsolicited promises.

"Whatever you need, just call."

"I'm here for you and the boys if you need help."

"No matter how late, don't hesitate to reach out."

"I'll stay in touch."

"What's your number? I'll call to check on you."

The reality is very few showed up. And that's okay.

Life happens for all of us, even when people have the best of intentions. One thing this journey has taught me is that people will make promises in the moment, but life will always get in the way. I've had to learn to free myself from the expectations of people and the things they promised.

Navigating my life as a widow meant that I had to learn to balance many things, keeping all the balls in the air at once. I went from having help shuttling the boys from place to place to *attempting* to do it on my own. Many times, things fell between the cracks. Opportunities were missed, activities were sometimes forgotten, and disappointed faces were my reward. I could only do so much with the resources of time and energy I possessed. Looking back, that was the only source of angst for me. Oftentimes, I would ask myself whether I gave each of my children exactly what they needed.

- *Did I spend enough time nurturing Jared's interests? Should I have enrolled him in the art classes or swimming lessons that he seemed to enjoy so much?*

- *Should I have let Kaelen quit soccer when he asked, especially when he was so good?*

- *Should I have allowed Jared to leave the Gifted and Talented program even though he seemed to be struggling to keep up?*

- *Should I have registered Kaelen for four AP classes instead of three, when he came home so late from track?*

Maybe to onlookers, I made it look *too* easy, especially on the highlight reels of social media. Many friends and family members who weren't there for the day-to-day would compliment me on how good Jared and Kaelen looked. *"They're so handsome. One looks just like you, and one looks like Raphie. You're doing a great job!"*

And for all intents and purposes, they were happy and healthy. On the outside, they appeared to be thriving. The reality was much different. Jared, like his dad, struggled with ADHD, and it was difficult to find a strategy that was successful. It took me many years to determine how to parent him. That I needed to give him grace for his struggle while holding him accountable for the things he needed to do. Many times, Kaelen wouldn't get the attention he needed from me, as I was preoccupied with ensuring that his brother was supported. I reasoned that Kaelen was adapting well and didn't need as much time from me since his grades were so good and he was a high-performing athlete. I provided tutoring, shuttled him to piano lessons, soccer games, and showed up for all the important moments.

But how does a parent ever know if what they're doing in the here and now is what's right for their children? The truth is, you won't. Not until much later. Life must play itself out. In the moment, you simply *do the best you can.*

As my boys grew, I began to feel the undeniable absence of their father in their lives. The culmination of all that I had done over the years never replaced the void that was left by losing him at such a young age. No matter how hard I tried to fill it. I knew I could never be what he would have been to them. I'm a mom. I was created differently.

What I chose to focus on instead was showing up for my children. Not being the "perfect" parent but being a "present" parent. Rarely allowing anything to distract me from what mattered most to my children because life is always evolving. What they needed at four, they didn't need at 14, and they'll need something else at 24, and so on.

> So, I finally learned to give myself grace for the journey. I learned that the best I could do was *the best I could do* because, frankly, *life be lifing,* and no matter what you say or do, there's nothing you can do to change that.

Lesson 6 Reflections

Date:_____

Today I Feel (Circle Your Choice):

1 - Joyful	2 - Happy	3 - Okay	4 - Sad	5 - Angry
😁	🙂	😐	🙁	😠

Today I'm grateful for:

_____

_____

_____

_____

Coloring Exercise "Blooming Vase": There's always a reason to hope because life unfolds in so many unexpected ways like the blooming of flowers.

Fig. 6. An AI-generated image of a bouquet of flowers in a vase.

Prompts: *Are there things that you've beat yourself about as you navigated your journey? I want you to reflect upon them long enough to let them go. Jot them down here and then cross through each one by one symbolizing the release of any guilt you have associated with them.*

_____

_____

_____

_____

_____

_____

_____

_____

_____

_____

_____

_____

_____

_____

Chapter 8

Lesson 7: Invest in your own healing.

A few months after Raphie's death, we visited a facility called Bo's Place. It was recommended by a colleague who felt we could benefit from the services they offered. Bo's Place is a center for families dealing with the loss of a loved one. They offer bereavement support and therapy groups for the entire family.

So, for about four weeks, I would load the boys into the car and drive across town for 35 minutes in terrible evening traffic to participate in their support groups. The boys were four at the time, so it's likely they don't even remember us going.

There were people from all walks of life, but very few who looked like us. We stood out like a sore thumb. In my head, I thought, *"Don't Black people go to grief support groups? Why are there so few of us in this room?"* Undeterred, because of the kindness they displayed toward me and the boys, I chose to be an "only" in the room. I reasoned, *This is what the boys and I need right now. It doesn't matter if there's no one here who looks like us—grief is personal. If they can help us, we need to be here.*

What I appreciated about Bo's was that they tried to match you with a group that could best relate to your circumstances. After a brief orientation, they whisked the boys off to a kid's group where they would play and color and have a great time with other kids their age. I was ushered into a room with other widows ranging in age to talk about the pain of our new lives.

Sitting quietly in the room, I listened to women sharing their pain in various stages of grief. Their stories varied from sudden death to watching a loved one die after a prolonged illness. I remember how hard it was to be in that room. I didn't yet feel comfortable talking about my grief with a room full of strangers. I didn't feel connected to them. I also wasn't falling apart at the time. I felt grounded in my faith. I had already railed at God, and I was doing better. I now know it was too soon for me to talk about what had happened to me; I don't think I was ready.

As I listened to story after story about the pain of losing a spouse, I began to think, "This is too much."

I stuck it out as long as I could, but by the fourth week, I'd had enough. I told them that the drive was too far, and we were done.

It would be several years before I ever sought out anyone else to talk about my loss. Instead, I went to church faithfully each week, spoke to my sisters often, and talked to great girlfriends about the goings-on in my life.

I was healing nicely.

I deserved to be in the Hall of Fame of widowhood. Sitting with Oprah under her oaks, teaching other women how to navigate grief and loss. I had this thing down.

Even though I hadn't had another meltdown since the first anniversary of Raphie's death, I wasn't ready to move forward with my life as a single woman. It had been three years, and I still hadn't taken off my wedding rings or removed Raphie's photo from the mantle. I wasn't interested in dating or even entertaining the thought of dating. It actually made me feel sick to my stomach when my best friend brought it up to me the first time. I knew I was faking it with everyone, assuring them that I was fine when in reality, I was stuck. Such is the gift of self-awareness. A part of me realized that if I ever wanted to feel like myself again or if I ever wanted to find love again, I had to talk to someone.

Beyond telling people what you need is realizing that you, and you alone, are in charge of your healing.

Seeking out therapy is not only brave, it's smart. There's no shame in getting the help you need. Recognizing that you need an impartial person to help you process your grief is what will eventually lead to your healing. The mere act of talking about my loss lightened the load for me. I can honestly say it was one of the best things I did for myself.

Losing someone you love is a *trauma,* and it will impact you mentally, emotionally, and physically. You will likely carry invisible scars from this trauma for a long time unless you stop to acknowledge and confront it.

So, my advice to you—take the reins of your healing. Don't try to go it alone or push it to the side. It will only delay what you need the most.

I'm so glad we now live in a time where we've normalized therapy and destigmatized its role in our lives.

> Your healing will not only help you, but it will help you show up better for those who most rely on you. So, try out a few different options until you find what works best for you. Whether it's a support group, a counselor, a life coach, or a spiritual healer. Just be sure the person you entrust your healing to is experienced and well-trained in helping you navigate the grieving process. Vet them carefully because placing your care in the wrong hands could do more harm than good.

In the end, embarking on this healing journey will be one of the best lessons you can learn in your life. One I'm sure will serve you again and again.

Lesson 7 Reflections

Date:_____

Today I Feel (Circle Your Choice):

1 - Joyful	2 - Happy	3 - Okay	4 - Sad	5 - Angry
😃	☺	😐	☹	😠

Today I'm grateful for:

_____

_____

_____

_____

_____

Coloring Exercise "In Your Hands": Even if you're struggling with feeling isolated and alone as you navigate this grief journey, this image is a reminder that your healing is in your hands.

Fig. 7. An AI-generated image of a black woman meditating.

Prompts: *Have you been trying to go it alone and suffering in silence? How is that manifesting in your life? Do you feel ready to seek professional help?*

Chapter 9

Lesson 8: Fall in love with who you are without your partner.

One day, I woke up and looked at the empty pillow beside me and realized, *"I need to redo this room so I can change the energy around me."* I had been stuck for a while, but I knew that it was finally time for me to move forward, whatever that now looked like for me.

Raphie and I had purchased our home together, so making changes to it was hard, but I knew I had to do it for my own sanity.

I wanted the rooms to be about me and the boys and what made us feel comfortable in our new lives without looking around all the time at what was. Raphie wasn't here anymore, and I had to create a space that reflected what we needed, or I knew I would end up selling our home. The boys loved our home, and I didn't want to have to uproot them from all that they had come to love, so the next best thing was to give them a newly renovated house that was still home.

The hardest part of this process was putting away or donating some of Raphie's things. I don't recommend that you do this alone but enlist the support of a friend or family member. Someone you know will help you navigate this emotional and difficult process. Yolanda helped me Marie Kondo everything as I parted with all of Raphie's things until eventually everything was packed away or donated and I was ready to begin the process of transforming our home.

So that's exactly what I did. I began renovations that would make any HGTV host proud. I put together a plan, created mood boards, selected swatches of materials and paint colors, and purchased new appliances before hiring a series of contractors to gut and redesign my home into the haven that I needed it to be. I spent hours at Lowes and Home Depot until they knew me by name. Working with contractors, from granite specialists to carpenters, for two months, I transformed the bedrooms, bathrooms, and kitchen into what the boys and I needed for our new lives. The result was a beautiful haven that we now call home.

It also became abundantly clear that I needed to rediscover the person I had become without a partner—reclaiming the essence of who Franka was—a woman tasked with crafting a vibrant life for her reshaped family.

Rediscovering my sense of self was imperative because I had suddenly transitioned from being one half of a couple to being a single woman. Alongside mourning my husband's loss, I was grieving the identity I had forged as a married woman. Most, if not all, of my friends were married, leaving me feeling like an outsider and, in many ways, the odd woman out. I was half of a couple on paper, yet "uncoupled" in reality. Mrs. Baly in name, but Ms. Baly in truth. Widowed, single, and alone.

So, I embarked on a journey of self-discovery, an odyssey to reintroduce me to ME. This undertaking was necessary as an integral part of my healing journey to prevent me from remaining trapped in the past.

Love might have left a gaping hole in my heart, but I knew that I owed it to myself to unearth what I now desired for my transformed life.

So, falling in love with myself included . . .

- Spending time rediscovering my hobbies.
- Trying new things, even if they didn't make financial sense to anyone else because I was doing them for the sheer joy of it.
- Investing in regular self-care rituals such as massages and facials. I made sure to budget them for myself at least once a month, knowing it was a part of my health and not a luxury.
- Organizing my living spaces to suit my tastes in terms of color, layout, and art. Those things brought my newly renovated home to life.

- Traveling to destinations that Franka always wanted to visit. I created my own bucket list that I'm still going through to this day.
- Creating a plan for my life centered around my own joy.
- Centering rest instead of always having to be "moving," even if that meant I missed out on career or financial opportunities.

> Learning to fall in love with a new version of yourself is a process. One that constantly requires reevaluation on your journey to self-discovery and self-love. It's important to find out what you want for your new life without your partner. This may require you to tap into long-forgotten dreams. *Are there things about who you were before you were married / in partnership that you now have to reacquaint yourself with?*

It's a radical act of self-love to spend time excavating that part of your life because it's likely that when you merged your life with your beloved, you adapted to a different rhythm. A couples' rhythm.

It's time to find a new rhythm. It's time to find *your* rhythm.

For me, it was all worth it to undergo the process of falling in love with myself, as today I'm able to easily move in the direction of *my dreams*. It has also given me knowledge and awareness of what makes me happy, and that has granted me a peace that surpasses all understanding.

Lesson 8 Reflections

Date:_____

Today I Feel (Circle Your Choice):

1 - Joyful	2 - Happy	3 - Okay	4 - Sad	5 - Angry
😄	🙂	😐	🙁	😠

Today I'm grateful for:

_____

_____

_____

_____

Coloring Exercise "My Haven": This is a reminder that you have the right to turn your space into exactly what you need it to be for your own sense of peace and well-being. Create your happy place.

Fig. 8. An AI-generated image of a luxurious bedroom.

Prompts: *Are you living the life you always imagined for yourself (even if it has evolved some over the years)? How can you honor what you need at this point in your life? What changes do you need to make to your life to reflect your dreams and what YOU want?*

Chapter 10

Lesson 9: Don't make big financial decisions when you're grieving.

I've made a few terrible financial decisions in my life, most of them when I was grieving. I didn't know there was a term for it—"grief shopping."

According to John Cappello, the author of *Open the Mind Heal the Heart*, "Grief shopping is an expression of your emotions attempting to balance the sadness you are feeling. It's an opportunity to learn about yourself."

It isn't always negative, and it can have some positive effects as long as you practice good judgment.

Although some of my decisions were rooted in positive motives, I didn't always think through each decision well enough due to grief shopping. In my case, this was due to my need to distract myself as I tried to cope with my loss.

Here are some of the bonehead moves I made.

- I opened an office in Downtown Houston right before the recession hit. I had to close it a year later since downtown looked like a ghost town, and no one wanted to come to the office.
- I opened a hair salon with a partner that I didn't properly vet. We had different ideas about how to run the salon, and she ended up leaving me to unload the entire investment on my own.
- I loaned money to a friend who had a history of not being trustworthy. Even though I saw her exhibit questionable behavior with others, I thought since we had always had a good relationship, I just knew she wouldn't take advantage of our friendship. I was wrong. What Maya Angelou says is true, "When people show you who they are, believe them the first time."

I can blame grief, but the truth is, I shouldn't have been making **any** financial decisions when I didn't have control of my emotions. I see that now. I tried and failed to fill a void that was left by the loss of my partner.

I love being needed and helping people; it's my kryptonite. But in this case, I needed to be *still*. Some people prey on vulnerability, so it's important to be discerning. If I'm honest with myself, it was not smart to make those investments. I've kicked myself many times about it a lot. Money that should have gone to take care of me and my boys went to people and projects that were unworthy of the investment.

The upside? It was a Masterclass in navigating finances after grief and loss, and the lessons I learned from it have stayed with me til this day.

So, what's my advice now?

- Take care of your basic needs, but don't make any major purchases for a year.
- Focus on creating consistency and continuity in your home life. You've just been through a drastic change, and you don't want to make another life-altering decision.
- Stick to a budget. If you do receive a large sum of money, spend like nothing changed for a while. Depending on your age and situation, you'll need to do some long-range financial planning to ensure that your resources will support you for the time you need.
- Say "No" to anyone who asks for money. Anything you have is for you and your immediate family and your own needs. You don't know how many years you have left on earth, and any funds are meant to help you live that life.
- Put any additional funds into an account that can accrue interest for you. Consult with a banker if you're not sure what type of account to set up.
- Create a will. Make sure if you have young children that you create a trust for them. There are so many

advantages to this. Speak to an attorney to help you set it up correctly.
- Get life and disability insurance. It will be invaluable if something happens to you, or if you're unable to work. Plus, with a life insurance policy, you can set it up as a trust to take care of your family in the event anything happens to you.
- Put all important paperwork or documents in a fireproof safe in a secure place in your home (wills, trust documents, passports, social security cards, birth certificates, bank accounts, etc.)
- Have all important items appraised for value. You need to know your net worth. If you ever have a catastrophic event, this information will come in handy.
- If your home was purchased jointly, you will need to refinance it to put it in your name.
- Make sure you get copies of the death certificate so you can send it to all of the utility companies so all bills come in your name. Have your spouse's name removed.
- If you own a business, get the appropriate amount of insurance to cover any project work and create a continuity plan.
- If your children are young, open 529 education accounts for each of them so the interest will compound and grow. Before you know it, they'll be going off to college, and you'll need money to help them as they navigate their lives as young adults.
- Maintain good credit or create a plan to repair it if you have issues with it. A good credit score is so important to wealth building, and its importance shouldn't be minimized. There are many great resources for

financial planning online these days, so don't go it alone if this is an area you struggle with.

My goal as my sons' only living parent was to make sure I did not create additional financial hardship for them if anything happened to me. After losing my husband so suddenly, my awareness of the impermanent nature of life was heightened, and I was not willing to leave anything to chance. To this day, I know it was the most loving thing I could do for them as their mom.

> Had I not made those financial mistakes in the past, I would not have done so many things right for my future or for theirs. Those lessons, although hard and painful at the time, taught me how tightly emotions and finances are intertwined and that it's important not to make any major financial decisions when you're grieving the loss of a loved one.

I'm grateful that this perspective now informs who I am today and equips me as I guide my sons into a more informed and bright financial future.

Lesson 9 Reflections

Date:_____

Today I Feel (Circle Your Choice):

1 - Joyful	2 - Happy	3 - Okay	4 - Sad	5 - Angry
😀	🙂	😐	🙁	😠

Today I'm grateful for:

_____

_____

_____

_____

Coloring Exercise "Serenity": Serenity and calmness are two emotions I felt when I saw this image. As you color, I hope you'll feel the same sense of peace and calm.

Fig. 9. An AI-generated image of a serene lake.

Prompts: *Are there any financial decisions you made or are considering making that you can now see are due to your grief? Have you made any purchases that you now recognize as grief shopping? How will you now proceed with this newfound awareness?*

Chapter 11

Lesson 10: Love has everything to do with it.

One of the things I most remember about Raphie was his laugh. It traveled straight from his diaphragm and belted out with a loud, "Ha, haaaaaaaaaaaaaa." Like a virus, it would infect every pore of your being. Before long, you would be laughing too, unable to stop yourself.

I used to tell him he had an embarrassing laugh. That I would have to hide so no one would know that it was coming out of his 5'9" frame. The memory of his laugh was a reminder of who he was at his core—a happy yet complicated person.

Despite any challenges we faced as a couple, and we had our share of ups and downs, I knew that I was loved *deeply*. Once my initial anger at God and at Raphie subsided, I reflected back a lot on who he was. I thought about our upbringing, our family dynamics, all the amazing things he had done for me and with me, and I knew, if no one else did, that I was greatly loved. The knowledge of this love is why I started to focus on what was the most loving way to honor his memory.

I would often ask myself...

- What do I want for my life now?
- What would Raphie want for me?
- What would he want for his boys?
- What could I do now that would evoke that wonderful laugh of his?

I knew him well enough to understand that the answers to these questions would lead me to a place of joy and contentment because he truly wanted the best for me. I understand that now more than ever.

Every day, I was given the opportunity to live a life that honored who Raphie was to me and the life I knew he would want for me and our boys. We had discussed child rearing, discipline, religion and so much more. The week before his passing, he shared an article with me about a set of twins who had won scholarships to college. Education was important to both of us, and I was determined to ensure that our children got a good one. We'll discuss later how God laughed at this plan.

In this life, I've often been reminded that even though tragic things happen to good people, it's how you choose to respond to the tragedy that matters. The choice is always there to respond with more gratitude and grace.

I have refused for my life to be defined by grief and loss. It was only a part of our story. What came before was much bigger. Like his laugh. As I reflected back on the years before and the happier times, I remembered all the trips we took. To places like Jamaica, France, Mexico, and Germany where we made memories of a lifetime. Or the wonderful conversations we had about "the state of Black people in America" and how we wanted to make a positive impact on the world—never running out of things to say. Our love of entertaining our friends and family for the holidays, birthdays, and other joyous occasions. All the incredible career highs we experienced and celebrated, from getting promotions at work to when I started my company, ReEmergence. The day I told him we would be having twins!! To the day we brought them home from the hospital. How I sobbed in his arms when Muddah died. And how he sobbed in mine when his dad lost his battle to prostate cancer.

We grew up together—experiencing the fullness of life.

Even though Raphie's chapter was over, mine was not. I still had chapters to write, and I knew that this was my season to lean into writing it.

Having lost both my parents as a young woman, my dad at 59 and my mother at 64, I thought I had internalized this lesson already, but somehow, losing my husband at 40 reinforced the concept of *living in the moment* more profoundly.

> As this realization hit me, I silently promised myself that I would do just that. *"Tomorrow isn't promised, Franka. You have to L-I-V-E. You get to decide what the rest of your life looks like. You get to decide how much joy you experience despite what has happened to you."*

From the moment I internalized this belief, I've tried to focus on learning all I could about living a happier life. I've become a student of it. From consuming books on positive psychology to getting my coaching certification, all the decisions I've made up to this point were part of my quest to tap into the joy I wanted for my life. The joy that I knew I deserved.

The beauty in navigating through the grief process is that it teaches you about who you are and what you're made of. You've already lost so much, so it feels like there's no place else to go but up.

Today, I'm certain that who I am and how I've raised my boys honors Raphie and what he meant to us. When I look at Kaelen and Jared, I see the kind, compassionate, and beautiful human beings they are. In my heart, I know their dad would be proud of them.

Even though education has remained important to me, it has looked different for each of my children. While Kaelen has gone off to college to pursue a degree in psychology, Jared has been steadfast in his refusal to attend. I've had to adjust to what they now say they want for their own lives.

What we want for our children doesn't always align with the dreams they have for themselves. Raphie didn't get to see this part of their evolution in their lives or the changes that our educational system has undergone in the past 15 years. The world looks different now, and there are many paths to success that didn't exist before. I firmly believe that my children will arrive at their own destination of "success" and however they define it, in their own way. My job is simply to be there to love and support them.

A month ago, Kaelen, Jared, and I were dancing to a song that we love. I can't even remember what it was, but I remember the smiles on our faces and, of course, the infectious laughter. At that moment, I could almost see Raphie smiling down on us. I realized that even though he's no longer with us in person, the essence of who he was will always be with us in the small, beautiful ways that matter because *love* has everything to do with it.

Lesson 10 Reflections

Date:_____

Today I Feel (Circle Your Choice):

1 - Joyful	2 - Happy	3 - Okay	4 - Sad	5 - Angry
😃	☺	😐	☹	😠

Today I'm grateful for:

_____

_____

_____

_____

Coloring Exercise "The Butterflies": In the Native American culture butterflies are a symbol of **transformation, hope, and rebirth**. What a beautiful reminder of what awaits you at the end of your grief journey.

Fig. 10. An AI-generated image of butterflies and flowers.

Prompts: *In what ways has your loved one left a mark on your life for the better? How has it shaped your perspective on living in the present and embracing joy?*

Chapter 12

Lesson 11: Sometimes you have to be your own cheerleader.

Raphie was one of my biggest cheerleaders. If I cooked us a meal, he would exclaim how great it was. If I decorated our home for friends to visit, he would tell me how beautiful everything looked. When I designed a web project, he never failed to tell me how much he admired my talent or how he loved my work ethic and attention to detail. Somehow, he took it upon himself to encourage me in everything I did, bragging to anyone who would listen that I was the smartest woman in the world. It was like a hit of dopamine.

That type of faith and encouragement boosted my confidence, and I was driven and audacious. During our marriage, I consistently used my talents in the service of others.

Bitten by the entrepreneurial bug early in life, I manifested every great idea that popped into my head during my marriage. Raphie had a front-row seat to the launch of my first company, EduQuest, an educational consulting company. And then again, when I launched ReEmergence, the first genesis of my design firm. He was my first investor and consultant. He advised me on how to grow and scale the business, even though I didn't always listen.

He had a brilliant financial mind and could run the numbers in his head for sales calculations and projections. I never cared about those things; I just wanted to be creative and help others, but running a business was hard, and it took everything out of me in those days. There was no social media or YouTube, no easy way to get your brand or message out there. It required grit, hard work, lots of networking, and a positive mindset.

Yet, Raphie somehow always knew when I was floundering and needed a pep talk. One day when I was having a particularly challenging time growing the company, he brought home a copy of the poem "Our Deepest Fear" written by Marianne Williamson from her book A Return to Love. At the time, he misattributed it to Nelson Mandela. It reads...

Our deepest fear is not that we are inadequate.
Our deepest fear is that we are powerful beyond measure.

*It is our light, not our darkness
That most frightens us.*

*We ask ourselves
Who am I to be brilliant, gorgeous, talented, fabulous?
Actually, who are you not to be?
You are a child of God.*

*Your playing small
Does not serve the world.
There's nothing enlightened about shrinking
So that other people won't feel insecure around you.*

*We are all meant to shine,
As children do.
We were born to make manifest
The glory of God that is within us.*

*It's not just in some of us;
It's in everyone.*

*And as we let our own light shine,
We unconsciously give other people permission to do the same.
As we're liberated from our own fear,
Our presence automatically liberates others.*

Once I finished reading it he told me, "Read this to remind yourself of your greatness and why it's important to always believe in yourself."

The next week, I landed a contract designing server training for HP. It would become one of the most lucrative contracts

I've ever had in my life, infusing hundreds of thousands of dollars into my business. So, it should come as no surprise that, to this day, that poem holds a special place in my heart.

When Raphie died, it meant that I lost my cheerleader. The person who was there for all the messy and hard parts but also the wins. He had been there for me to lean on, and he had encouraged me daily. Family and friends are a distant substitute for this kind of intimate companionship. Even though they consistently called to check on me, I was never able to burden them with my day-to-day struggles or how I was navigating my new reality alone. I didn't want them to worry unnecessarily because somehow, in my spirit, call it intuition or faith, I knew I would figure it out one day.

And figure it out I did, but it took a long time, and I made a lot of mistakes along the way. As I mentioned previously, that strong Black woman trope is a part of who I am. That type of internal wiring doesn't fall away easily; it takes time. In those early years of becoming a widow, I still thought I had to figure it out alone. I didn't quite yet know about the work of Dr. *Brené* Brown or the concept of being built for community and connection.

So, how did I become my own cheerleader?

As I navigated my new life as a widow, I began to appreciate the power of silence and the importance of sitting with my own thoughts. In the quiet moments, answers to questions or situations I had been struggling with would come to me. I started noticing patterns of when I would get these answers, and they frequently came when I was in the shower or out for a walk in nature.

So, water and nature became my conductors. They grounded me and realigned my mind. I realized that once I shut out the everyday noise, I could tap into my own power and find a peace that would permeate my life.

I could more clearly hear from God, and sometimes I imagined I could also hear the voices of Mother or Daddy. At times, I could also hear Raphie giving me advice. I couldn't actually hear their voices, but I could imagine what they would say to me.

Then one day, out of nowhere, it hit me, *"I'm doing okay. Even if no one is watching or no one can hear, I can cheer on myself. I can encourage myself."*

There's a beautiful gospel song by Sheri Jones-Moffett, called, "Encourage Yourself." I've saved it on my Spotify playlist, and I play it whenever I need a reminder.

Here are some of the lyrics:

Sometimes you have to encourage yourself
Sometimes you have to speak victory during the test
And no matter how you feel
Speak the word, and you will be healed
Speak over yourself
Encourage yourself in the Lord

Sometimes you have to encourage yourself
Gotta pat yourself on the back.

Sometimes you have to speak victory during the test
And no matter how you feel
Speak the word over your life
Speak the word, and you will be healed
Speak over yourself
Encourage yourself in the Lord

Sometimes you have to speak a word over yourself
Depression is all around
But God is present help
Well, the enemy created walls
But remember giants, they do fall
Speak over yourself
Encourage yourself in the Lord
As I minister to you, oh I minister to myself
Life can hurt you so
'Til you feel there's nothing left
No matter how you feel
Speak the word over your life, and you will be healed
Sometimes you gotta look yourself in the mirror
And tell yourself, "I can make it"
You gotta remember that's life's a death lock in the power of your own tongue
Even if nobody tells you, you can run on
You tell yourself

You gotta remember, I'm more than a conqueror
Hey, where there is weakness in me
I believe everything that the Lord said about me
Everything the enemy ever told me, it's a lie, it's a lie
I will lift up mine eyes unto the hills.

> So powerful, right? The line that always moves me is, "Life's a death lock in the power of your own tongue." So, knowing what to say to yourself in those quiet moments is crucially important to your mental health. Speak great things over yourself, regardless of whether anyone else can hear. You will hear, and that's what's most important.

Learning this lesson of how to encourage myself not only enhanced my life but also made me aware of a strength I didn't even know I possessed. I've had to grow and stretch myself to become the woman I am today. Raphie's absence from my life built a reliance on God as my constant confidant. To this day, I credit learning this lesson for helping me navigate all that life has thrown my way, and for that, I'm beyond grateful.

Lesson 11 Reflections

Date:_____

Today I Feel (Circle Your Choice):

1 - Joyful	2 - Happy	3 - Okay	4 - Sad	5 - Angry
😄	🙂	😐	🙁	😠

Today I'm grateful for:

_____

_____

_____

_____

Coloring Exercise "The Joy of Life": A reminder that there is so much joy in life. I believe you will reconnect to your joy again after dealing with your profound loss. You will laugh out loud again.

Fig. 11. An AI-generated image of a woman laughing joyfully.

Prompts: *It is likely that your beloved did things for you that have left a void in your life now that they're gone. What are some ways you can encourage yourself every day to help fill the void?*

Chapter 13

Lesson 12: It's important to say one final goodbye.

I believe one of the most important aspects of the grieving process is getting closure. I have heard some say that it's not necessary, I disagree. I've experienced both options and I experienced closure with Mother but not with Daddy, and I struggled after his passing. There was so much left unsaid, and I think I was even mad at Daddy before he died. I had not had much communication with him after I left for college. He died in my freshman year of college, and it was sudden and jolting. At the age of 59, he had a fatal heart attack. The circumstances of his death were vague to me because we had been told he was improving, but then overnight in the hospital, they lost him. No explanation. He was gone.

When my dad passed, everything I thought I was mad about didn't even matter. All I knew was that I lost my Daddy. The man who spun me around gleefully as a child and who was the most dominant male figure in my life.

When Raphie died, I also didn't get closure.

His head injuries were so severe that I was encouraged not to view his body. I was told to remember him as he was. I decided to comply. His casket was closed at the funeral. A familiar hollow feeling in the pit of my stomach was there. The same feeling I'd had years earlier when I didn't get closure with Daddy.

Over the years, I've been torn about my decision not to view Raphie's body. Mostly because it delayed the process of closure for me. As a military wife, my thoughts often went to all the wives whose husbands were killed in action or who never got to see their loved ones again. Their only solace, a carefully wrapped American flag or their beloved's dog tags. When I reflected on their grief, I was able to not feel sorry for myself for a time. I tried to reason that life is unpredictable and unfair, and we don't always get what we want, and that the pain of loss is a part of this human journey. This worked for a time. But no matter how much logic your brain understands about what you *should* be feeling, the heart does what it *wants*.

I *still* struggled.

For a long time, I felt anger because I felt cheated in saying that final goodbye, and then it morphed to sadness because I didn't get to look upon his face one last time. I now know that seeing him battered and bruised beyond recognition would not have been a good final memory for me, and I'm glad I trusted my intuition not to view him that way.

With the support of my therapist many years later, I was encouraged to get the closure I needed by writing a letter to Raphie. So, despite it being many years later, I sat down at my desk and wrote him one final letter. A full stream of consciousness of what I was feeling. After I finished the letter, I sealed it and tucked it away in my nightstand. It was there for several years until the day I knew the time had come for me to part with it. I went into the backyard and lit it on fire on my concrete patio. I watched as it was consumed until it was nothing but ashes. As the ashes blew in the wind, I knew in my heart I had finally gotten the closure I needed. I was finally free, and I wanted to start anew without feeling like I was in emotional quicksand.

> I believe the act of writing that letter freed me in many ways. I've been able to think about my years as a wife without tying them to the enormous loss I suffered. Although loss was a part of my story, it was not the entire story. Getting to say one final goodbye allowed me to fully express everything I was feeling at that moment and gave me the closure I so desperately needed. In my heart, I know that's what Raphie would want for me.

Here are some prompts to help you write your own letter.

> Tell them how much you miss them.
> I never expected you to . . .
> I'm mad at you for . . .

You're going to miss...
This wasn't a part of our plan.
Once again, you've gotten out of . . .
I feel guilty for . . .
I hope you didn't . . .
I will remember . . .
I will love . . .

When you sit down to your write, the words will come. Just remember, it's about getting the closure you deserve and need so you can move forward with the life you're meant to live.

Lesson 12 Reflections

Date:_____

Today I Feel (Circle Your Choice):

1 - Joyful	2 - Happy	3 - Okay	4 - Sad	5 - Angry
😄	🙂	😐	🙁	😠

Today I'm grateful for:

_____

_____

_____

_____

Coloring Exercise "A New Day": A reminder that on the grief journey there will come a day when you will look forward to the promise of a new day with hope, expectation, and gratitude like the rising of the sun.

Fig. 12. An AI-generated image of the sun rising over the ocean.

Prompt: *Write a letter to your loved one to say the things you wished you could have if your loved one was still here. After you're done, seal the letter. Below, jot down some ideas to include in the letter, even if you're not ready to write the letter yet. Your thoughts will be here when you're ready.*

Chapter 14

Final Thoughts

"And when great souls die, after a period, peace blooms, slowly and always irregularly. Spaces fill with a kind of soothing electric vibration. Our senses, restored, never to be the same, whisper to us. They existed. They existed. We can be. Be and be better. For they existed."

- Maya Angelou

The concept that *love never dies* means that even though your beloved is no longer alive to share your life, the memory of that love will live forever in your heart, and it will bring you happiness and joy as you remember how deeply you were once loved in this life.

Time is a gentle healer, gradually soothing the ache of your loss. As the days flow, some memories, too, find their way into the river of time. It's the little things that will linger.

For me, it was the sweet fragments of love and laughter. Or the way Raphie's eyes lit up with pride when I did something great. Or the shared belly laughs we had while watching an episode of *Martin, Frasier,* or *A Different World.*

Mementos, photographs, and videos, though painful in the beginning, now bring a smile to my face. They give life to the nuances of our colorful love story.

Life's lessons, sometimes shouting, other times whispering—oftentimes appearing in dreams. Dreams, where Raphie has remained suspended in time, just as he was. Waking is a bittersweet return to reality. I embrace this reality, yet at times, it's a weight to carry. I cherish our dreams, footprints in the sands of time and in my mind—hopefully never fading with time.

With the years has come perspective—an unveiling of who Raphie was and the love we shared. It echoes in the laughter of our children, reflections of him mirrored in each of them in a special way. His legacy has left an indelible mark on each of us.

I've been focused of late on creating a vibrant, joy-centered life filled with adventure as I continue my attempt at balancing the roles of both mother and father. Hoping to fill up space in my children's lives big enough for two people.

Today, the prospect of marrying again, although a distant hope, is not a priority. My children have grown into young adulthood, and so too has my perspective on being alone. I continue to navigate a changed landscape of dating and connection.

But I remain open to the possibility of love's return. If you have loved before, there is always the possibility to love again. It is outside of my control, but I remain open to receiving all that God has for me.

I view my life as a blessing and gratitude as my anchor. Every achievement, every accomplishment, is a testament to a life gifted, not merely happened. Even though the tale we began was cut short, my story continues.

One certainty is true in this uncertain life—Raphie, though physically absent, resides in the eternal sanctuary of my heart. *Why?* Because love transcends the boundaries of time and space. **Love is immortal, a melody that never dies.**

Final Reflections

Date:_____

Today I Feel (Circle Your Choice):

1 - Joyful	2 - Happy	3 - Okay	4 - Sad	5 - Angry
😄	🙂	😐	🙁	😠

Today I'm grateful for:

_____

_____

_____

_____

_____

_____

Prompt: *What is your hope for your future?*

In Loving Memory

Raphael Alexander Baly
Oct 4, 1966 - May 27, 2008

This is one of my favorite photos of Raphie—laughing his infectious laugh.

My Family Album

Below are some pictures of my life with Raphie and the life that my sons and I built after his passing. As difficult as it was at the beginning of our journey, we have built a vibrant, joy-filled, and amazing life. Yes, we've had some challenging moments on this journey but through it all God has shown us grace and favor.

If you're recently beginning your grief journey, it may be difficult to even imagine smiling again, let alone building a life filled with so much adventure and joy. I hope my story encourages you and you believe in your own resilience and strength to navigate your journey through grief and loss.

Life with Raphie on p. 107 (from left to right): (1) Raphael with our boys Jared and Kaelen, (2) Raphie and I celebrating my 30th birthday, (3) With the boys on their 2nd Christmas, (4) Raphie and I on our wedding day, (5) On our first cruise, (6) on vacation in The Bahamas, (7) At Essence Festival in New Orleans, (8) Enjoying my favorite band Mint Condition (9) Enjoying a 7-course meal in Paris, France, (10) Enjoying San Francisco, CA (11) Freezing in Munich, Germany.

The Rebuilt Life on p. 108 (from left to right): (1) Enjoying the Aquarium, (2) Celebrating the boys' 8th birthday, (3) Riding to school, (4) Boys hanging out on the wharf in St. Croix, (5) Remaking a moment from Home Alone, (6) On our way to Nice, France, (7) Freezing in Rockefeller Plaza in NYC, (8) Enjoying a day on the Riverwalk in San Antonio, (9) Soccer days at the YMCA, (10) Hiking to the top of Diamondhead, Hawaii, (11) Christmas at home, (12) Hanging out at home, (13) A day cheering for the Houston Dynamo, and (14) the boys' first Homecoming Dance.

Citations

American Heart Association, (2022, May 4). *Is Broken Heart Syndrome Real?* Retrieved October 18, 2023 from https://www.heart.org/en/health-topics/cardiomyopathy/what-is-cardiomyopathy-in-adults/is-broken-heart-syndrome real#:~:text=The%20most%20common%20signs%20and,occur%20with%20broken%20heart%20syndrome.

Cappello, J. (2016). *Open the Mind Heal the Heart* (1st ed., p. 208). BalboaPress.

Ibeh, C. (2020, September 25). *Chimamanda Adichie: 10 Powerful Quotes on Grief and Mourning.* Brittle Paper. Retrieved October 18, 2023, from https://brittlepaper.com/2020/09/chimamanda-adichie-10-powerful-quotes-on-grief-and-mourning/.

Lynn, L. (2022, February 23). *When Great Souls Die.* AfterTalk. Retrieved October 18, 2023, from https://blog.aftertalk.com/when-great-souls-die-aftertalk-inspirational-2-23-22/.

Stansbury, L., & Aman, M. (2022, December 20). *56 Powerful Quotes About Grief to Get Anyone Through the Hard Times.* Woman's Day. https://www.womansday.com/life/g37793747/grief-quotes/.

Williamson, Marianne, (1992). *A Return to Love: Reflections on the Principles of A Course In Miracles* (1st ed., p. 190). HarperOne.

Acknowledgments

I'm eternally grateful to . . .

To God for being the source of everything. For carrying me through the highs and lows of this journey, even when I couldn't see my way through. You kept me, and I'm eternally grateful.

The team at Get It Done, LLC, and the Tiny Book Course for the information, knowledge, support, and encouragement as I birthed this book. Through the gift of their scholarship, I was able to stay committed to the writing process in order to create a book that deserved to be in the world.

All my brothers and sisters, but especially Gloria and Marilyn. Thank you for always encouraging me and pouring into me. Your love and kindness helped me to become the woman that I am today. Thank you for being on this journey with me and never leaving my side. You embody the word "family" to me.

To Raphie's family, especially his Mom, Sheila and his siblings, Joyce, Alex and Andrae for being there for me and supporting me throughout the years.

My dear friend Kirleen, who is more like a sister than a friend. Thank you for always listening and challenging me to show up vulnerably and authentically. You've been on this journey with me through the good, the bad, and the ugly. Thank you for always being my soft place to fall.

My friend Korey, for being my accountability partner as I embarked on this journey. Thank you for checking in on me as I tried to squeeze in writing through my workload and all the demands of life.

Thank you to my girlfriend circle and The Girlfriend Gathering Bookclub; Miara, LaShanna, Tera, Markena, Pamela, LaGina, Tameka, Carol, Kiambre, Neika, and Phyllis. Through our regular discussions about love and life, you've helped me unearth the courage to share all that I am today. Thank you for showing up with your authenticity and heart.

My amazing parents, Theodora and George Nicholas, for giving me life and for pouring into me how to be a woman of integrity, kindness, and love. You let me explore with wonder and love and ignited that creative spark in me that lives to this day. I live my life to make you proud. Thank you for all the sacrifices you made to give me all the opportunities I've had in this life.

My dear Raphie. Thank you for being a part of my life for so many years and for being one of my greatest teachers. I hope you are resting well in the knowledge that I have embodied the love that we shared with our boys. Our love never died; it merely transformed.

About the Author

Franka J. Baly is a designer, researcher, and dream launcher. She is the Creative Director of Franka Baly Media, LLC. For the past three decades, she has worked as a visual brand strategist and user experience designer - a UX Brand Strategist (a term she coined herself). She helps both large corporations and small business owners create research-informed and engaging user experiences aligned with their branding. Simultaneously, she's been on a mission to empower women to live inspired and joy-filled lives, especially as they evolve in life. She does this by supporting them in launching a personal or business brand aligned with their purpose and passion. Now with more than 100 brands and websites under her belt, she has a deep commitment to amplifying diverse female voices in the digital landscape. Franka is a native of the island of Trinidad but grew up on the island of St. Croix, and currently lives in Tomball, Texas with her two sons. To connect with Franka visit her at her website: frankabaly.com.

www.ingramcontent.com/pod-product-compliance
Lightning Source LLC
Chambersburg PA
CBHW050733010526
44107CB00010B/828